Down through the Roof

Mark 2:1–12 and Luke 5:18–26 for children

Written by Jeffrey E. Burkart • Illustrated by Paige Billin-Frye

Arch® Books
Copyright © 1999 Concordia Publishing House
3558 S. Jefferson Avenue, St. Louis, MO 63118-3968
Manufactured in Colombia

Straight to His home away from home
Our dear Lord Jesus once did roam.
And people came from miles around
To see Him in Capernaum town.

We think that Jesus went to stay
In Peter's house upon the day,
When Jesus chose to help someone
Who couldn't jump and couldn't run.

There was a man upon a bed
Who couldn't move; he looked half-dead.
And to the house this man was brought
By four good friends who were distraught.

They worried that their friend might die,
So to the house the men drew nigh
In hopes that Jesus Christ could mend
The sickly body of their friend.

The house was crowded as could be,
And those outside could hardly see.
They pushed and shoved and strained all day
To hear what Jesus had to say.

No matter how very hard they tried,
The men just could not get inside.
The house was full! There was no way
For them to get inside that day.

So they devised a brilliant plan.
Up to the roof they brought the man,
And through that roof of sticks and clay,
They dug a hole without delay.

Lord Jesus faced the man and spoke.
He said, "Son, listen, it's no joke!
Your sins are all forgiven now!"
But some who heard Him thought, "Oh, wow!

"Who can forgive but God alone?
He has blasphemed, that's clearly shown!
Why does this fellow talk like this?
We're sure that something is amiss!"

But Jesus knew each secret thought,
And so, our Lord and Master taught
A lesson to each person who
Forbade the things that He might do.

He said, "Why do you think this way?
You think it's easier to say,
'Your sin's erased' 'cause it's just talk,
Or 'Get up, take your bed, and walk'?

" 'We all know talk is cheap,' you say,
So I will prove to you this day
The Son of Man has got the right
To grant forgiveness day and night.

"Get up, now, take your bed, and walk!"
And what He said was not just talk.
The man who couldn't move before
Got up and walked right out the door.

Then in full view of those around,
He picked his bed up off the ground.
And all who saw it were amazed
As each one to the Lord sang praise!

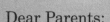

Dear Parents:

This well-loved Bible story tells the account of four men, desperate to help, who dug a hole in the roof and lowered their paralyzed friend into a crowded room. What faith they displayed!

Some of those present were horrified to hear Jesus tell the physically paralyzed man that his sins were forgiven. They criticized Jesus, saying, "Only God can forgive sins!" Jesus challenged them by asking, "Which is easier: to say to this man, 'Your sins are forgiven,' or 'Take up your bed and walk'?" The point Jesus was making is that both are impossible for people but equally easy for God.

This miracle and others display the deity of Jesus. We, too, can use the miracles of Jesus to teach our children about the glory of God. When they are fascinated with the "magic" of the miracle, remind them that miracles are not magical tricks of the eye, but something only God alone can do. Miracles show that Jesus truly is the Son of God, the promised Messiah who took away the sins of the world—the greatest miracle of all!

The Editor